VOLUME 3

She

delighting in the examples
of the women of the Bible

Delight Thyself
DESIGN MINISTRIES

delightthyself.com

Copyright © 2022 by Delight Thyself Design Ministries, Inc.

All Scripture quotations are taken from the King James Bible.

Published by Delight In Him Publications,
a division of Delight Thyself Design Ministries in Hurricane, WV.

The mission of Delight Thyself Design Ministries is to design and distribute the printed Word of the Gospel of Jesus Christ.

All rights reserved. No part of this book may be reproduced or transmitted in any form or by any means electronic, mechanical, photocopy, recording, or otherwise without the written permission of the publisher, except for brief quotations in online or printed reviews.

Delight Thyself Design Ministries, Inc.
PO Box 725
Hurricane, WV 25526
delightthyself.com

The contents of this book are the result of years of spiritual growth in life and ministry. Every effort has been made to give proper credit and attribution to quotes and information that is not original. It is not our intent to claim originality with any quote or thought that could not be tied to an original source.

Printed in the United States of America.

ISBN: 978-0-9995175-4-3

*To each of the Godly ladies
who have pointed me to His Word.*

Galatians 6:9

Also Available

Delight Thyself Also In The Lord:
a simple daily devotional

Delight Thyself Also In The Lord:
a simple daily devotional - Volume 2

Order My Steps In Thy Word:
a verse by verse study of Psalm 119

She:
Delighting In The Examples Of The Women Of The Bible

Volume 1	Volume 2
Abigail	Anna
Bathsheba	Eve
Deborah	Hannah
Lydia	Jochebed
Martha	Mary Magdalene
Mary Of Bethany	Naomi
Michal	Pharaoh's Daughter
Phebe	Ruth
The Syrophenician Woman	Sapphira
The Virtuous Woman	The True Harlot Mother
The Widow Of Zarephath	The Widow With Two Mites
The Woman In The City	The Woman With An Issue Of Blood

Releasing Soon

She:
Delighting In The Examples Of The Women Of The Bible

Volume 4
Delilah
Esther
Hagar
Herodias
Lot's Wife
Miriam
Rebekah
Sarah
The Maid By The Fire
The Queen Of Sheba
The Widow With Oil
The Woman With A Spirit Of Infirmity

VOLUME 3
The Women of the Bible

Elisabeth	9
Gomer	15
Leah	21
Mary The Mother Of Jesus	27
Rachel	41
Rahab	47
Rhoda	55
Tabitha	61
Tamar	67
The Shunammite Woman	73
The Widow Of Nain	79
The Woman In Adultery	85
Be A Woman Of The Bible	91
References	95
The Bible Way To Heaven	104

She...

The series of **She** consists of four volumes, each focusing on the lives of 12 women of the Bible. Many of the women are familiar, some less spoken of, but each are applicable to our lives today.

The objective of this series is not an effort to reveal some new theory about the women, but simply to point us to the pages of the Word of God so that the Lord can speak to us as only He can. Ask Him to show you the Truths found within the testimonies of each of these women that He has preserved for us to read.

Symbols:

The leaves around a name signify the beginning of the study of a new woman.

SHE...
This shows us a quality that we can apply to ourselves, or seek to become.

SHE...
This denotes a fact about them as women during their time in history.

Read
A suggested passage for the context of the study.

Memorize
Verse(s) to help apply the characteristics of the woman.

Apply
A question or two to encourage you to dwell on what can be learned from the example of the woman of the Bible.

Elisabeth

Read: Luke 1

Luke 1:36

"...she hath also conceived a son in her old age..."

SHE WAS THE COUSIN OF MARY THE MOTHER OF JESUS.

Luke 1:36

"And, behold, thy _____ Elisabeth, she hath also conceived a son in her old age: and this is the _____ month with her, who was called _____."

Mary conceived as a virgin.

SHE CONCEIVED IN HER OLD AGE.

Luke 1:37

"For with God _____ shall be impossible."

SHE WAS ALSO WITH CHILD WHEN MARY CAME TO VISIT HER.

Luke 1:41-42

"And it came to pass, that, when Elisabeth heard the _____ of Mary,

the babe _____ in her womb;

and Elisabeth was _____ with the Holy Ghost:

And she spake out with a loud voice, and said,

Blessed art thou among women, and blessed is the _____ of thy womb."

SHE WAS OVERWHELMED THAT THE MOTHER OF JESUS WAS IN HER HOUSE.

Luke 1:43

"And whence is this to me,

that the mother of my Lord should _____ to me?"

SHE WAS HUMBLE.

She heard Mary, and the babe leaped with joy that Jesus was near.

Luke 1:44

"For, lo, as soon as the _____ of thy salutation sounded in mine ears, the babe leaped in my _____ for joy."

She was filled with the Holy Spirit.

She...

Elisabeth serves as an example of how the presence of the Lord brings joy to those around Him.

Memorize:
Psalm 16:11
"Thou wilt shew me the path of life: in thy presence is fulness of joy; at thy right hand there are pleasures for evermore."

Apply:
Mary came to Elisabeth in her time of need. Who is an Elisabeth in your life?

_____

May we all seek to be an Elisabeth to someone else.

Who was Elisabeth's son?

_____

Notes

Gomer

Read: Hosea 2 & 3

Hosea 2:6

"...she shall not find her paths."

Hosea 2:6

"Therefore, behold, I will hedge up thy way with _____, and make a wall, that she shall not find her paths."

SHE LEFT HER HUSBAND, AND SUFFERED THE CONSEQUENCES.

Hosea 2:7

"And she shall follow after her lovers, but she shall not _____ them; and she shall seek them, but shall not _____ them: then shall she say, I will go and _____ to my first husband; for then was it _____ with me than now."

SHE LEFT HOSEA, AND BECAME A SLAVE.

Hosea 2:15

"And I will give her her vineyards from thence, and the valley of Achor for a door of _____: and she shall _____ there, as in the days of her youth, and as in the day when she came up out of the land of Egypt."

SHE LEFT HOSEA, BUT HE LOVED HER STILL.

Hosea 3:1

"Then said the LORD unto me, Go yet, love a woman beloved of her friend, yet an _____, according to the love of the LORD toward the children of Israel, who look to other gods, and love flagons of wine."

He redeemed her back to himself.

Hosea 3:2

"So I _____ her to me for fifteen pieces of silver, and for an homer of barley, and an half homer of barley:"

SHE IS A PICTURE OF THE NATION OF ISRAEL THAT WAS SEPARATED FROM JUDAH, BUT SHE IS ALSO A PICTURE OF US.

When we were lost in our sin, our own Door of Hope came and redeemed us back when we could not save ourselves.

She...

GOMER SERVES AS AN EXAMPLE OF HOW JESUS CHRIST LOVES US AND WANTS TO REDEEM US.

Memorize:
1 Corinthians 6:20
"For ye are bought with a price: therefore glorify God in your body, and in your spirit, which are God's."

Apply:
How has Jesus Christ redeemed us?

_____

_____

_____

Notes

Leah

Read: Genesis 29

Leah

Genesis 29:35

"...she called his name Judah..."

SHE WAS LABAN'S FIRSTBORN DAUGHTER, WHO HAD A SISTER NAMED RACHEL.

Genesis 29:25

"And it came to pass, that in the morning, behold, it was _____: and he said to Laban, What is this thou hast done unto me? did not I serve with thee for Rachel? wherefore then hast thou _____ me?"

SHE BECAME JACOB'S UNPLANNED FIRST WIFE.

Jacob fell in love with Rachel the moment he saw her, and worked for their father seven years before he was to wed Rachel.
Instead, Laban deceivingly sent Leah to be Jacob's wife.

SHE WAS NOT THE ONE HE HAD WANTED.

Jacob loved her less than he loved Rachel.

Genesis 29:30-31

"And he went in also unto Rachel, and he loved also Rachel _____ than Leah, and served with him yet _____ other years. And when the LORD saw that Leah was _____, he opened her womb: but Rachel was barren."

Though she was loved less, the Lord granted her children first.
She had given birth to Reuben, Simeon, and Levi before she had her fourth child, Judah.
His name means praise.

Jacob may have loved Rachel more because of her outward beauty, but it was Leah whose inner beauty allowed God to choose her to birth the son of Jacob from whose line Jesus Christ came.

God saw her heart.
She suffered the pain of being second choice,
yet the Lord chose to use her in a great way for His glory.

1 Samuel 16:7

"...for the LORD _____ not as man seeth;

for man looketh on the outward appearance,

but the LORD _____ on the heart."

Leah serves as an example that God does not look on our outward appearance, but rather He looks upon our hearts.

Memorize:
Proverbs 31:30
"Favour is deceitful, and beauty is vain: but a woman that feareth the LORD, she shall be praised."

Apply:
How can you apply Leah's character to your life?

_____

_____

_____

Notes

Mary The Mother Of Jesus

Read: Matthew 1

Matthew 1:18

"...she was found with child of the Holy Ghost."

SHE WAS A VIRGIN, YET SHE WAS WITH CHILD.

Matthew 1:18

"Now the _____ of Jesus Christ was on this wise:

When as his _____ Mary was espoused to Joseph,

_____ they came together,

she was found _____ child of the Holy Ghost."

Matthew 1:23

"Behold, a virgin shall be with _____,

and shall bring forth a _____,

and they shall call his name _____,

which being interpreted is, God _____ us."

SHE WAS THE VESSEL GOD CHOSE TO FULFILL THE PROPHECY SPOKEN OF BY ISAIAH.

Isaiah 7:14

"Therefore the Lord himself shall give you a _____ ; Behold, a virgin shall conceive, and bear a son, and shall call his name _____."

SHE WAS CONFUSED AT FIRST.

Luke 1:34

"Then said Mary unto the angel, _____ shall this be, seeing I know not a man?"

Have you ever been so confused that you asked God, "how?" or "why?"

She was overshadowed by the Holy Ghost.

Luke 1:35

"And the angel answered and said unto her,
The _____ _____ shall come upon thee, and the _____ of the Highest shall overshadow thee: therefore also that holy _____ which shall be born of thee shall be called the _____ of God."

She remained pure until she gave birth to Jesus.

Matthew 1:25

"And knew her not till she had brought forth her _____ son: and he called his name _____."

She...

Mary the Mother of Jesus serves as an example that nothing is impossible with God.

Memorize:
Luke 1:37
"For with God nothing shall be impossible."

Apply:
Why is the virgin birth of Jesus Christ so important?

_____

_____

_____

Read: Luke 1:26-38

Mary The Mother Of Jesus
Matthew 1:21

"...she shall bring forth a son..."

She carried the Saviour of the world into this world for a specific purpose.

Matthew 1:21

"And she shall bring forth a son, and thou shalt call his _____ JESUS: for he shall _____ his people from their _____."

She was espoused to Joseph.

The angel of the Lord appeared unto him in a dream telling of what was going to take place.

Matthew 1:20

"But while he _____ on these things, behold, the angel of the Lord appeared unto him in a _____, saying, Joseph, thou son of David, _____ _____ to take unto thee Mary thy wife: for that which is conceived in _____ is of the Holy Ghost."

She was highly favoured.

Luke 1:28

"And the angel came in unto her, and said, _____, thou that art highly favoured, the Lord is with thee: _____ art thou among women."

She heard of His greatness.

Luke 1:32

"He shall be _____, and shall be called the Son of the _____: and the Lord God shall give unto him the _____ of his father David:"

Luke 1:33

"And he shall _____ over the house of Jacob for ever;

and of his _____ there shall be no end."

SHE WAS WILLING.

Luke 1:38

"And Mary said, Behold the _____ of the Lord;

be it unto me _____ to thy word. And the angel departed from her."

How willing are we?

She...

MARY THE MOTHER OF JESUS ALSO SERVES AS AN EXAMPLE THAT GOD CAN USE US FOR A SPECIFIC PURPOSE.

Memorize:
Psalm 40:8
"I delight to do thy will, O my God: yea, thy law is within my heart."

Apply:
What did it mean when Mary said "...*be it unto me according to thy word*..."?

_____

_____

_____

Read: Luke 1:39-56

Mary The Mother Of Jesus
Luke 1:45

"...she that believed..."

SHE BELIEVED.

Luke 1:45

"And _____ is she that believed:

for there shall be a _____

of those _____ which were told her from the Lord."

SHE WAS WILLING.

Luke 1:38

"And Mary said, Behold the handmaid of the Lord;

_____ _____ _____ _____

according to thy word. And the angel departed from her."

**Her willingness was birthed in faith
that if the Lord said it,
there is no doubt it would happen.**

Hebrews 11:6

"But without _____ it is _____ to please him:

for he that cometh to God must _____ that he is,

and that he is a _____ of them

that _____ seek him."

SHE HAD FAITH,
AND GOD PERFORMED A MIRACLE.

Philippians 1:6

"Being _____ of this very thing,

that he which hath _____ a good _____ in you

will _____ it until the day of Jesus Christ:"

Mary the Mother of Jesus also serves as an example that when we believe what the Lord has promised, He is certain to perform it.

Many of our prayers appear to go unanswered
simply because we do not believe that God is willing and able to bring it to pass.

Cast out the doubt today, and choose to believe that God is Able.

Memorize:
Psalm 37:4-5
"Delight thyself also in the LORD;
and he shall give thee the desires of thine heart.
Commit thy way unto the LORD; trust also in him;
and he shall bring it to pass."

Apply:
What miracle are you asking and believing He will perform?

_____

_____

_____

Read: Luke 2:1-6

Mary The Mother Of Jesus
Luke 2:6

> "...she should be delivered."

SHE HAD CARRIED JESUS IN HER WOMB FOR THE REQUIRED TIME.

Prophecy had been declared that Christ would be born in Bethlehem.

Micah 5:2

"But thou, _____ Ephratah, though thou be _____ among the

thousands of Judah, yet out of thee shall he _____ forth unto me

that is to be _____ in Israel; whose goings forth

have been from of old, from _____."

SHE AND JOSEPH WERE IN GALILEE, IN THE CITY OF NAZARETH.

Caesar Augustus made a decree that all were required to pay taxes.

Luke 2:1

"And it came to _____ in those days,

that there went out a _____ from Caesar Augustus,

that all the _____ should be taxed."

Because he was of the lineage of David,
this required Joseph to return to Bethlehem.

Luke 2:4-5

"And _____ also went up from Galilee, out of the city of Nazareth,

into Judaea, unto the city of _____, which is called Bethlehem;

(because he was of the house and _____ of David:)

To be taxed with _____ his espoused wife, being _____ with child."

Luke 2:6

"And so it was, that, while they were there,

the days were _____ that she should be delivered."

She...

Mary the Mother of Jesus also serves as an example of how Christ will guide our steps to exactly when and where He desires us to be.

Memorize:
Proverbs 16:9
"A man's heart deviseth his way: but the LORD directeth his steps."

Apply:
How has the Lord directed your steps before?

_____

_____

_____

Read: Luke 2:7-20

Mary The Mother Of Jesus
Luke 2:7

> "...she brought forth her firstborn son..."

She was whom the Lord chose to use to bring the Word into the world.

John 1:14

"And the Word was made _____, and dwelt among us, (and we beheld his _____, the glory as of the only _____ of the Father,) full of _____ and_____."

She gave birth to Jesus.

Luke 2:7

"And she brought _____ her firstborn son, and wrapped him in _____ clothes, and laid him in a _____; because there was no _____ for them in the inn."

She wrapped Him in swaddling clothes.

They were grave clothes, which signified His purpose.

Luke 2:11

"For unto you is _____ this day in the city of David a _____, which is _____ the Lord."

She laid Him in a manger.

Regardless of whether or not there is room made for Him, the Lord will carry out His purpose. Think of everything that innkeeper missed out on because he rejected Joseph and Mary that night.

She was visited by the shepherds.
They were told of the birth of Jesus by the angel of the Lord.

Luke 2:17

"And when they had seen it, they made _____ abroad

the _____ which was told them concerning this child."

**While they made Him known,
she pondered all that God had done through her.**

Luke 2:19

"But Mary _____ all these things,

and _____ them in her _____."

She...

MARY THE MOTHER OF JESUS ALSO SERVES

AS AN EXAMPLE OF THE GREAT THINGS

THAT ARE POSSIBLE THROUGH US

IF WE WILL SIMPLY YIELD OURSELVES TO THE LORD.

Memorize:
1 Samuel 12:24
"Only fear the LORD, and serve him in truth with all your heart:
for consider how great things he hath done for you."

Apply:
Why would Mary ponder these things?
Take time today to ponder what He has done for you.

_____

_____

_____

Notes

Rachel

Read: Genesis 30 & 35

Genesis 35:16

"...she had hard labour."

She went through a season of barrenness.

Genesis 30:1

"And when Rachel saw that she bare Jacob _____ children, Rachel _____ her sister; and said unto Jacob, Give me children, or else I die."

She blamed her husband for her despair.

She was the one whom he loved, yet she had not bare him any children.

Genesis 30:2

"And Jacob's anger was _____ against Rachel: and he said, Am I in God's stead, who hath _____ from thee the _____ of the womb?"

Much like her grandmother-in-law, she decided to take matters into her own hands rather than waiting on the Lord to provide.
Genesis 30:3-6

She ended up with two sons by Bilhah, Dan and Naphtali.
Their names remind us that God judged and heard Rachel's prayer
in the midst of the great struggle within and around her.
After that trial of waiting, God remembered Rachel and gave her children.

Genesis 30:22

"And God _____ Rachel, and God hearkened to her, and _____ her womb."

She gave birth to Joseph with faith of another son.

He would be the portrait of Christ in the Old Testament
for every generation afterward to read and learn from.

| 43

Genesis 30:23-24

"And she conceived, and _____ a son; and said,

God hath taken away my _____: And she called his name Joseph;

and said, The LORD shall add to me _____ son."

She gave birth to Benjamin.
This was after Jacob's name changing experience in Bethel.

Genesis 35:16

"And they journeyed from _____; and there was but a little way

to come to Ephrath: and Rachel _____, and she had hard labour."

She would experience hard labour,
and end up naming her son while drawing her last breath.
Genesis 35:17-18

She...

Rachel serves as an example that what we seek and eventually find may end in sorrow, but God always has a purpose & will for our lives.

Memorize:
2 Corinthians 4:17
"For our light affliction, which is but for a moment,
worketh for us a far more exceeding and eternal weight of glory;"

Apply:
How has the Lord used sorrow in your life for your good and His glory?

_____

_____

Notes

Rahab

Read: Joshua 2:1-15

Joshua 2:15

"...she let them down by a cord through the window..."

She was a harlot in Jericho.

Joshua 2:1

"And Joshua the son of Nun sent out of Shittim two men to _____ secretly, saying, Go view the land, even _____. And they went, and came into an harlot's house, named _____, and lodged there."

She lied to protect the men she hid.

Joshua 2:4-5

"And the woman took the two men, and _____ them, and said thus, There came men unto me, but I _____ not whence they were: And it came to pass about the time of shutting of the gate, when it was _____, that the men went out: whither the men went I wot not: _____ after them quickly; for ye shall overtake them."

She had heard what the Lord did for them.
Joshua 2:10-11

She had faith.
Joshua 2:12

"Now therefore, I _____ you, swear unto me by the LORD, since I have shewed you _____, that ye will also shew kindness unto my father's house, and give me a _____ token:"

She believed that if she protected the men of the Lord, she would also receive protection.
Joshua 2:13-14

| 49

SHE HID THEM, AND THEN LET THEM DOWN SAFELY THROUGH THE WINDOW BY A CORD.

Joshua 2:15

"Then she let them down by a _____ through the window: for her house was upon the town _____, and she dwelt upon the wall."

She...

RAHAB SERVES AS AN EXAMPLE THAT WHEN WE BLESS THE PEOPLE OF GOD, HE WILL BLESS US IN RETURN.

Memorize:
Genesis 12:3
"And I will bless them that bless thee, and curse him that curseth thee: and in thee shall all families of the earth be blessed."

Apply:
What was the *"true token"* that Rahab requested?

_____
_____
_____

Read: Joshua 2:16-24
Joshua 6:15-19

Rahab

Hebrews 11:31

"...she had received the spies with peace."

Hebrews 11:31

"By _____ the harlot Rahab perished not with them that _____ not, when she had received the spies with peace."

SHE LET THE SPIES DOWN THE WALL TO SAVE THEIR LIVES.
The scarlet thread in the window saved her and her family.

Joshua 2:18

"Behold, when we come into the land, thou shalt bind this line of _____ thread in the window which thou didst let _____ down by: and thou shalt bring thy father, and thy mother, and thy brethren, and all thy father's household, _____ unto thee."

SHE WAS SAVED BY FAITH.

Joshua 2:21

"And she said, According unto your _____, so be it. And she sent them away, and they departed: and she bound the scarlet _____ in the window."

Imagine what she must have felt as she heard the people
shout after their seventh time around the city.
She could have been fearful, but instead she had peace.

Joshua 6:16-17

"And it came to pass at the _____ time, when the priests blew with the trumpets, Joshua said unto the people, _____; for the LORD hath given you the city. And the city shall be _____, even it, and all that are therein, to the LORD: only _____ the harlot shall live, she and _____ that are with her in the house, _____ she hid the messengers that we sent."

| 51

She was saved for a purpose.

She was the mother of Boaz, who became the kinsman redeemer of Ruth.
She was the grandmother of Obed, their son.
She was the great-grandmother of Jesse, the father of King David.

Twenty-eight generations later, Jesus Christ was born in their lineage.
Her great faith preserved her family
so that the King of Kings could be born through her lineage many years later.

Rahab also serves as an example that faith in what we may consider to be small things leads to God doing great things in and through us.

Memorize:
Psalm 126:3
"The LORD hath done great things for us; whereof we are glad."

Apply:
What small thing has He made great in your life?

_____

_____

_____

Notes

Rhoda

Read: Acts 12

Acts 12:14

"...she opened not the gate for gladness..."

SHE DID NOT OPEN THE DOOR IMMEDIATELY.

Peter had just been miraculously released from prison by the angel of the Lord.

Acts 12:12

"And when he had _____ the thing, he came to the house of Mary

the mother of John, whose surname was _____;

where many were gathered _____ praying."

He came to Mary's house and knocked on the door
behind which there were many praying for him to be released.

Acts 12:13

"And as Peter _____ at the door of the gate,

a _____ came to hearken, named Rhoda."

Their answer to prayer was literally knocking on the door of the house.

SHE WAS A SERVANT.

Acts 12:14

"And when she knew Peter's _____,

she opened not the gate for gladness,

but _____ in, and told how Peter stood _____ the gate."

SHE KNEW HIS VOICE.

It was familiar to her for she must have heard him preach often,
yet she was too stunned to do the most logical thing.

Instead of opening the door to let him in, she ran to tell the others
that the Lord had granted their request. The very thing they had prayed for
had happened, and she was overwhelmed with gladness and joy.

Acts 12:15

"And they said unto her, Thou art _____.

But she constantly _____ that it was even so. Then said they, It is his angel."

**SHE GAVE THE PRAISE REPORT,
BUT THEY DID NOT BELIEVE HER.**

The knocking continued,
perhaps getting louder and louder to prove he was outside.

SHE HAD TOLD THEM, BUT THEY HAD TO SEE FOR THEMSELVES.

Acts 12:16

"But Peter _____ knocking: and when they had opened the door,

and saw him, they were _____."

She...

RHODA SERVES AS AN EXAMPLE OF THE GLADNESS AND JOY THAT WE CAN RECEIVE WHEN THE LORD ANSWERS OUR PERSISTENT PRAYERS.

Memorize:
Matthew 7:7-8
"Ask, and it shall be given you; seek, and ye shall find; knock, and it shall be opened unto you: For every one that asketh receiveth; and he that seeketh findeth; and to him that knocketh it shall be opened."

Apply:
What are you persistently praying about?

_____

_____

Notes

Tabitha

Read: Acts 9:32-43

Acts 9:37

"...she was sick, and died..."

SHE WAS KNOWN FOR HER GOOD WORKS.

Acts 9:36-37

"Now there was at Joppa a certain _____ named Tabitha, which by interpretation is called Dorcas: this woman was full of _____ works and _____ which she did. And it came to pass in those days, that she was sick, and died: whom when they had _____, they laid her in an _____ chamber."

SHE WAS ALSO CALLED DORCAS.

Acts 9:39

"Then Peter _____ and went with them. When he was come, they brought him into the upper chamber: and all the _____ stood by him weeping, and shewing the coats and _____ which Dorcas made, while she was with them."

SHE WAS KNOWN FOR HER SEWING AND GENEROSITY.

SHE WAS FAITHFUL UNTO DEATH.

Acts 9:40-41

"But Peter put them all forth, and kneeled down, and _____; and turning him to the body said, Tabitha, arise. And she _____ her eyes: and when she saw Peter, she _____ up. And he gave her his hand, and lifted her up, and when he had called the saints and widows, presented her _____."

**Her friends sent for Peter,
and then witnessed a miracle because of her faithfulness.**

She was alive again,
a living testimony of the miraculous grace of God.

Acts 9:42

"And it was known throughout all _____;

and many _____ in the Lord."

She...

Tabitha serves as an example that faithfulness can lead to great miracles and much fruit.

Memorize:
Proverbs 31:10
"Who can find a virtuous woman? for her price is far above rubies."

Apply:
Faithfulness is a rare quality. How can you be more faithful?

_____

_____

_____

Notes

Tamar

Read: Genesis 38

Genesis 38:24

"...she is with child by whoredom..."

SHE ENDURED THE LOST OF TWO HUSBANDS.

Her first husband, Er, the son of Judah, did evil in the sight of the Lord and He slew him. Her second husband, Onan, refused to fulfill the Hebrew law of raising up a seed for his dead brother through Tamar. He also displeased the Lord and was killed.

Judah begged her to stay as a widow within her father's house.

Genesis 38:11

"Then said Judah to Tamar his _____ in law, Remain a widow at thy father's house, till Shelah my son be grown: for he said, Lest _____ he die also, as his brethren did. And Tamar went and dwelt in her _____ house."

Instead of doing what he had promised, Judah refrained from giving his third son to her to marry. When she realized this, Tamar took matters in to her own hands and disguised herself as a harlot by covering her face from Judah when he inquired of her.

Genesis 38:15

"When Judah saw her, he thought her to be an _____; because she had _____ her face."

She became pregnant with twins after her encounter with Judah, though he was unaware that it was his daughter in law at the time.

Genesis 38:24

"And it came to pass about _____ months after, that it was told Judah, saying, Tamar thy daughter in law hath _____ the harlot; and also, behold, she is with child by whoredom. And Judah said, Bring her forth, and let her be _____."

Judah commanded her to be burnt when he first realized the news, but then later realized that she in fact was more righteous than he when compared to the evil that he had done. He was now the father of the second set of twins recorded in Scripture.

She gave birth to Zarah and Pharez.
Genesis 38:27-30

Zarah had a scarlet thread bound to his hand.
Pharez was the second born, but it was through his lineage that our Saviour was born.

Judah was a Jew; and Tamar, a Gentile.
What a beautiful picture of foreshadowing that both Jews and Gentiles can share in the blessings of the Gospel.

Matthew 1:1-3

"The book of the generation of _____ _____, the son of David, the son of Abraham. Abraham begat _____; and Isaac begat _____; and Jacob begat Judas and his _____; And Judas begat Phares and Zara of _____; and Phares begat Esrom; and Esrom begat Aram;"

She...

Tamar serves as an example of how God can overcome the sin we commit and give victory through His Son and our Saviour, Jesus Christ.

Memorize:
1 Corinthians 15:57
"But thanks be to God, which giveth us the victory through our Lord Jesus Christ."

Apply:
How has God given you victory through Jesus Christ?

_____

_____

Notes

The Shunammite Woman

Read: 2 Kings 4

The Shunammite Woman

2 Kings 4:8

> "...she constrained him to eat bread..."

2 Kings 4:8

"And it fell on a day, that Elisha passed to _____,

where was a _____ woman;

and she constrained him to eat bread.

And so it was, that as _____ as he passed by,

he turned in thither to _____ bread."

She perceived that Elisha was a man of God.

2 Kings 4:9

"And she said unto her _____, Behold now,

I perceive that this is an _____ man of God,

which _____ by us continually."

**She must have seen him often to know
that he passed by their way frequently.**

She saw the opportunity to do something for him that would honor the Lord.

2 Kings 4:10

"Let us make a little _____, I pray thee, on the wall;

and let us set for him there a _____, and a _____,

and a _____, and a _____:

and it shall be, when he _____ to us, that he shall turn in thither."

SHE AND HER HUSBAND MADE A ROOM
SPECIFICALLY FOR ELISHA TO STAY IN WHEN HE WAS IN TOWN.

She...

THE SHUNAMMITE WOMAN SERVES AS AN EXAMPLE OF HOW IMPORTANT IT IS TO HONOR THOSE WHO FAITHFULLY SERVE THE LORD.

If we will honor God's people, He will honor us.

Memorize:
1 Corinthians 15:58
"Therefore, my beloved brethren, be ye stedfast, unmoveable, always abounding in the work of the Lord, forasmuch as ye know that your labour is not in vain in the Lord."

Apply:
How can you honor those the Lord has used in your life?

_____

_____

_____

Notes

The Widow Of Nain

Read: Luke 7:11-17

The Widow Of Nain
Luke 7:12

"...she was a widow..."

She was a widow, who had one son.

Luke 7:12

"Now when he came nigh to the _____ of the city,

behold, there was a dead man _____ out, the only son of his mother,

and she was a widow: and much people of the _____ was with her."

She received compassion from Jesus.

There is no record that anyone asked Him to help,
He simply reacted to her obvious sorrow.

Luke 7:13

"And when the _____ saw her,

he had _____ on her, and said unto her, *Weep not*."

She saw Jesus resurrect her son.

Luke 7:14-15

"And he came and touched the _____: and they that bare him stood still.

And he said, *Young man, I say unto thee, _____*. And he that was dead sat up,

and began to speak. And he _____ him to his mother."

Jesus touched the coffin that the Jews carried him in,
and simply commanded him to "*Arise.*"

Her son was the first person that Jesus raised from the dead.

The multitude of witnesses all rejoiced with godly fear
and glorified God for what Christ had done.

Luke 7:16

"And there came a fear on all: and they _____ God, saying,

That a great _____ is risen up among us;

and, That _____ hath visited his people."

This miracle caused the fame of Jesus to spread farther as people began to realize just Who He is.

Luke 7:17

"And this _____ of him went forth throughout all Judaea,

and _____ all the region round about."

She...

The Widow Of Nain serves as an example of the miracles that Christ can perform in our lives simply because of His love for us.

**When the Lord works miracles,
we must do just as the multitudes did that day…glorify Him.**

Memorize:
1 John 4:9
"In this was manifested the love of God toward us, because that God sent his only begotten Son into the world, that we might live through him."

Apply:
How can you use your testimony to glorify Him?

_____

_____

_____

Notes

The Woman In Adultery

Read: John 8:1-11

The Woman In Adultery

John 8:11

"She said, No man, Lord."

She was brought to Jesus by the scribes and Pharisees.

John 8:3-4

"And the scribes and Pharisees brought unto him a _____ taken in adultry; and when they had set her in the _____, They say unto him, _____, this woman was taken in adultry, in the very act."

She was found in the act of adultery, a crime punishable by death by stoning.

John 8:5

"Now Moses in the _____ commanded us, that _____ should be stoned: but what _____ thou?"

They used her to tempt Jesus.

John 8:6

"This they said, tempting him, that they might have to _____ him. But Jesus _____ down, and with his finger wrote on the _____, as though he _____ them not."

He ignored them at first, but they persisted.

John 8:7-8

"So when they continued _____ him, he lifted up himself, and said unto them, He that is without _____ among you, let him first _____ a stone at her. And again he _____ down, and _____ on the ground."

After Jesus spoke, her accusers departed one by one.
John 8:9

She could have fled like the convicted accusers, yet she remained.

SHE ENDED UP ALONE WITH JESUS.
Just her and Him.

John 8:10

"When Jesus had lifted up himself, and saw none but the woman, he said unto her,

Woman, where are those thine _____? hath no man condemned thee?"

She did not try to defend herself.
She simply answered His question while acknowledging Who He is.

John 8:11

"She said, No man, _____. And Jesus said unto her,

Neither do I condemn thee: _____, and sin _____ more."

SHE CALLED HIM LORD.
She became a new creature after her experience with Jesus.

She...

THE WOMAN IN ADULTERY SERVES AS AN EXAMPLE OF THE TRANSFORMATION THAT CAN TAKE PLACE WHEN WE ARE WITH JESUS.

Memorize:
2 Corinthians 5:17
"Therefore if any man be in Christ, he is a new creature:
old things are passed away; behold, all things are become new."

Apply:
How do we become *"a new creature"*?

_____

_____

Notes

Be A Woman Of The Bible

Be A Woman Of The Bible

Did you know that there are three distinct ways to understand the Bible?

Read
Deuteronomy 17:19

Search
John 5:39

Study
2 Timothy 2:15

You have studied the lives of 12 Women of the Bible.
Their names or testimonies are recorded on the pages of the Word of God for specific purposes. The characteristics of their lives are examples of the many things you can choose to apply to your life.

Although your name is not printed in the canon of the Scriptures, you can still be known as a Woman of the Bible by purposing yourself to use the qualities of their lives to affect how you walk with the Lord.

The Book of James describes two different choices you have
in your response to what you find in the Word of God.

James 1:22-25
"But be ye doers of the word, and not hearers only, deceiving your own selves.
For if any be a hearer of the word, and not a doer, he is like unto a man beholding his natural face in a glass: For he beholdeth himself, and goeth his way,
and straightway forgetteth what manner of man he was.
But whoso looketh into the perfect law of liberty, and continueth therein, he being not a forgetful hearer, but a doer of the work, this man shall be blessed in his deed."

LIVE OUT WHAT YOU KNOW.

If you are to be known as a woman who follows Biblical Truth,
you have to live out what you know.
"doers of the word, and not hearers only"

There is a difference between what you know and what you believe.

Many people who call themselves "Christians" know Biblical Truth.
They know that Jesus Christ was the Son of God.
They know that Jesus died on the cross.

They even know that He died on the cross of their sins.
They know a lot of things...but have they believed on Him?

**There is a difference in knowing something,
and actually believing, or placing your faith in it.**

Many have heard the phrase that "people can be 18 inches away from Heaven". The principle found here is so true.

Many know that Abraham Lincoln was the 16th President of the United States of America. Many even know that he famously spoke the Emancipation Proclamation, and that he led the abolishment of slavery.

They have never met him, yet they know many things about him.

There are many people that know countless facts about Who Jesus is, yet they have not placed their faith and trust in what He did on the cross for them.

That is the difference.

LIVE OUT WHAT YOU BELIEVE.

The same principle applies to the women you have studied throughout this book. You can know everything about their lives, so much so that you could clear the "Women of the Bible" column on the Jeopardy board, but if you do not apply what you know to your life it simply ends with knowledge.

You can know many many things found within the pages of God's Word, but if you only hear them without being a doer of those Truths, the Book of James clearly says that you are deceiving yourself.

Be A Woman Of The Bible

References

References

ELISABETH
"A Worshipper Of God"

LUKE 1:5-80

GOMER
"Completion"

HOSEA 1:1-11 & HOSEA 3:1-5

LEAH
"Wearied"

GENESIS 29; GENESIS 30; GENESIS 49:31; RUTH 4:11

MARY THE MOTHER OF JESUS
"Bitterness"

MATTHEW 1 & 2; MATTHEW 12:46; LUKE 1 & 2
JOHN 2:1-11; JOHN 19:25; ACTS 1:14

RACHEL
"Ewe"

GENESIS 29, 30 & 31; GENESIS 33:1, 2, 7; GENESIS 35:16-26;
GENESIS 46:19, 22, 25; GENESIS 48:7; RUTH 4:11; 1 SAMUEL 10:2;
JEREMIAH 31:15; MATTHEW 2:18

RAHAB
"Fierceness"

JOSHUA 2:1-3; JOSHUA 6:17-25;
MATTHEW 1:5; HEBREWS 11:31; JAMES 2:25

Rhoda
"Rose"
Acts 12:1-19

Tabitha
"Female Roebuck or Gazelle"
Acts 9:36-43

Tamar
"A Palm Tree"
Genesis 38:6-30; Ruth 4:12; 1 Chronicles 2:4
Matthew 1:3

The Shunammite Woman
2 Kings 4:8-37; 2 Kings 8:1-6

The Widow Of Nain
Luke 7:11-18

The Woman In Adultery
John 8:1-11

Notes

_____
_____
_____
_____
_____
_____
_____
_____
_____
_____
_____

About Us

About Us

*"Delight thyself also in the LORD;
and he shall give thee the desires of thine heart."*
Psalm 37:4

From this verse comes the inspiration behind the name of this ministry. It is a reminder that if we delight ourselves in Him, He promises to give us desires according to His will for our lives.

In 2012, the desire for a design ministry began. The Lord has since opened door after door to allow that desire to become a reality..."*Commit thy way unto the LORD; trust also in him; and he shall bring it to pass."* Psalm 37:5

Delight Thyself Design Ministries began as a media ministry at Teays Valley Baptist Church of Hurricane, WV. Then Lord directed us toward reaching people with the printed Word of the Gospel. A tract ministry was born, and has since continued to grow as the Lord leads. In 2014, we began shipping tracts to missionaries across the world with little or no material with which to reach their field. **Please pray with us** that the Lord will continue to provide resources to print the tracts the missionaries are requesting.

We ship tracts free of charge to anyone willing to distribute the printed Word of the Gospel of Jesus Christ. Contact us if you would like to receive a sample pack or box to distribute.

Gospel tracts customized with a church's contact information are a great way to spread the Gospel and allow others to contact your ministry. We also design custom material for Independent Baptist Churches, which helps fund the printing and distribution of Gospel tracts which are sent across the world.

We are so thankful for those whom the Lord has provided to support this ministry on a monthly basis or through one time donations. If it were not for the Lord using these generous people, this ministry simply could not exist today. We claim Philippians 4:17 for this method of support, *"Not because I desire a gift: but I desire fruit that may abound to your account."*

If you would like to receive ministry updates, follow us on social media or send us your email address to receive our newsletters.

Delight Thyself
DESIGN MINISTRIES

delightthyself.com

What Can One Tract Do?

One tract was sitting in the office of the home of a young man named, Hudson. When he found it, he read over it and the phrase "the finished work of Christ" began to work on his heart about his need for salvation. He then surrendered his life to Christ, and was burdened for the people of China. This man was who we now know as Hudson Taylor, the missionary who brought the Good News of the Gospel to China.

One tract was given by a friend to a man named Joe. Over the next several months, the Lord used that tract to put him under conviction, cause him to go to church and walk the aisle to trust Christ as His Saviour. When he got up, he saw his pregnant wife beside him. She had also came forward by faith to accept Christ. This is the testimony of the parents of the founder of this ministry. One tract led to their salvation, a Christian heritage, and the start of this ministry. Without God using a man to give that one tract, this ministry would not exist today.

One tract has now yielded over 3,500,000 tracts to date being sent all across the world, and only heaven will reveal the fruit that remains. To God be the glory, for great things only He hath done.

Isaiah 55:11
"So shall my word be that goeth forth out of my mouth:
it shall not return unto me void,
but it shall accomplish that which I please,
and it shall prosper in the thing whereto I sent it."

**Will you allow God to use you
to spread the printed Word of the Gospel?**

Visit delightthyself.com for more resources.

ONE TRACT
CAN
MAKE A
DIFFERENCE

The Bible Way To Heaven

*"Jesus saith unto him, I am the way, the truth, and the life;
no man cometh unto the Father, but by me."*
John 14:6

We Are All Sinners.
"For all have sinned, and come short of the glory of God."
Romans 3:23

We Were Sent A Saviour.
*"But God commendeth his love toward us, in that,
while we were yet sinners, Christ died for us."*
Romans 5:8

We Were Supplied A Gift.
*"For the wages of sin is death;
but the gift of God is eternal life through Jesus Christ our Lord."*
Romans 6:23

We Can Simply Confess & Call.
*"That if thou shalt confess with thy mouth the Lord Jesus,
and shalt believe in thine heart that God
hath raised him from the dead, thou shalt be saved.
For whosoever shall call upon the name of the Lord shall be saved."*
Romans 10:9,13

It's that simple.

The Bible says... **Whosoever.**
Once you see yourself as a sinner, if you will simply *"call upon the name of the Lord"*, you can be saved from spending eternity in the Lake of Fire separated from God. You may say..."It's not for me." or "I'll never be good enough.", but God said... **Whosoever.**

God is not willing that any should perish.
That includes you.

If you have trusted Christ as your Saviour,
or would like more information, please contact us.

delightthyself.com

www.ingramcontent.com/pod-product-compliance
Lightning Source LLC
Chambersburg PA
CBHW061154010526
44118CB00027B/2971